21st
Century
Skills Library

REAL WORLD MATH: NATURAL DISASTERS

TSUNAMIS

BY TAMRA B. ORR

Published in the United States of America by
Cherry Lake Publishing, Ann Arbor, Michigan
www.cherrylakepublishing.com

Content Adviser
Jack Williams
Founding editor of the *USA Today* weather page and author of *The AMS Weather Book: The Ultimate Guide to America's Weather*

Math Adviser
Katherine M. Gregory, M.Ed

Credits
Cover and page 1, ©Cryssfotos/Dreamstime.com; page 4, ©Rod Haestier/Alamy; page 7, ©Rex Features via AP Images; page 8, ©John Orsbun/Shutterstock, Inc.; page 10, ©Byelikova Oksana/Shutterstock, Inc.; page 12, ©Vicki D. Oseland/Dreamstime.com; page 14, ©AP Photo/Bullit Marquez; page 16, ©AP Photo; page 18, ©AP Photo/Rick Rycroft; page 20, ©ARCTIC IMAGES/Alamy; page 24, ©Cowardlion/Dreamstime.com; page 26, ©AVAVA/Shutterstock, Inc.

Library of Congress Cataloging-in-Publication Data
Orr, Tamra.
  Tsunamis / by Tamra B. Orr.
     p. cm.—(Real world math)
  Includes bibliographical references and index.
  ISBN 978-1-61080-327-4 (lib.bdg.)—ISBN 978-1-61080-336-6 (e-book)—
ISBN 978-1-61080-410-3 (pbk.)
  1. Tsunamis—Juvenile literature. 2. Mathematics—Juvenile literature. I. Title.
II. Series.
  GC221.5.O826 2012
  551.46'37—dc23   2011032522

Cherry Lake Publishing would like to acknowledge
the work of The Partnership for 21st Century Skills.
Please visit *www.21stcenturyskills.org* for more information.

Printed in the United States of America
Corporate Graphics Inc.
January 2012
CLSP10

TABLE OF CONTENTS

CHAPTER ONE
TERROR IN JAPAN

The people of Japan are familiar with earthquakes—and they should be. For generations, the country has been shaken by quakes of all sizes. In fact, Japan experiences about

Tsunami waves are much larger than the waves that normally occur.

20 percent of the world's largest earthquakes. Almost 100 years ago, a huge quake hit Kanto, a region on the main island of Honshu. It killed more than 140,000 people. Since then, almost four dozen major quakes have rocked the nation.

Many of these quakes were damaging, killing thousands of people and destroying countless buildings. But none of these natural disasters can compare to the underwater quake that struck on March 11, 2011, about 80 miles (129 kilometers) east of Sendai, on Japan's east coast. The quake ranks as one of the world's most powerful earthquakes in the last century.

For almost five minutes, the earth rattled and rumbled. The quake's force was so strong that experts believe it actually moved the island of Japan 8 feet (2.4 meters)! But it was not the brute power of the quake that brought massive devastation to the Sendai region. Instead, it was the **tsunami**, gigantic ocean waves, that followed.

The quake in the ocean was almost as intense as an exploding atomic bomb. The ocean floor was pushed down several feet, hurling billions of cubic yards of water out of place for hundreds of miles.

Boaters out on the ocean probably never noticed the slight bump of the tsunami wave as it rolled beneath them. Traveling at nearly the speed of a jet plane, the water raced toward Japan. Warnings to the people were made only 15 minutes before the wave hit shore.

But those who lived along Japan's coast already knew what was about to happen. They had felt the quake. They had seen the beaches suddenly empty of water as it was drawn back from the shoreline, leaving fish flapping on the wet sand. Tourists, however, were fascinated and curious at the ocean's sudden disappearance. Many flocked to the shore to take photographs. For some, it would be their last moments of life.

Suddenly, an enormous roaring sound came from the ocean. Astonished onlookers couldn't believe their eyes. A giant wall of water was growing bigger and louder with each passing second—and heading straight for the shore. People panicked. They frantically searched for a strong object to grab on to. Many ran to find higher ground.

When the tsunami finally made **landfall**, the wall of water was more than 33 feet (10 m) high, or taller than a three-story building. It destroyed everything in its path.

REAL WORLD MATH CHALLENGE

Living in Japan requires getting accustomed to earthquakes. Up to 2,000 quakes are felt each year. What is the average number of quakes per day? Per month?

(Turn to page 29 for the answers)

The tsunami and earthquake in 2011 caused incredible destruction throughout Japan.

"It's basically like a hundred tanks coming across you," explained **oceanographer** Philip Froelich. "Even though it's a fluid, it operates like a solid hammer."

Water poured through Sendai. It toppled buildings, tossed cars and trucks, and killed many people. Tsunami warnings were issued in many other parts of the world, including South America, Canada, Alaska, and Oregon. Wave after wave sped across hundreds of miles of ocean waters.

The effects of the earthquake in Japan were felt as far away as Maui, Hawaii.

The tsunami took the lives of more than 20,000 people and caused billions of dollars in damage. The disaster made it abundantly clear that water is one of the most powerful forces on the planet.

21ST CENTURY CONTENT

After the tsunami was over, the cleanup began. But months later, a large amount of debris still floated in the ocean. Experts at the International Pacific Research Center at the University of Hawaii determined the location of that trash and where it was heading. According to their predictions, one to two years after the tsunami the debris would arrive on Hawaii's shores. Ocean currents would carry in more trash a few years later. Nikolai Maximenko, a spokesperson for the center, said, "We live in Hawaii, on the edge of the biggest dump site in the world."

CHAPTER TWO
MOTHER NATURE'S SHOVE

Water is surprisingly heavy and has amazing power when in motion. If you doubt it, take a look at how the Colorado River carved solid rock into the Grand Canyon over millions of years. The moving waters of the river created a canyon that is 277 miles (446 km) long, up to 18 miles (29 km) wide, and 1 mile (1.6 km) deep.

A major volcanic eruption can create a tsunami that causes damage several miles away.

It isn't easy for Mother Nature to create a tsunami. There are only four events powerful enough to generate one: a volcanic eruption, an earthquake, an underwater or coastal landslide, and a meteor impact. The majority of tsunamis originate in the Pacific Ocean. But it is possible to have them in inland seas, such as the Baltic and Caspian Seas, and in very deep lakes.

The earth is covered with a thin outer shell made of huge, slowly moving pieces called **tectonic plates**. When one plate grinds against another, it can cause an earthquake. If the earthquake occurs in the ocean, and is strong enough, it can create a tsunami. The quake literally shoves the water, which begins moving at amazing speeds of up to 700 miles (1,127 km) per hour. When the wave reaches the shore, the water on the bottom slows down because of **friction**. The water higher up is still moving quickly and piles up, creating a wall of water that can flatten trees, houses, and buildings.

REAL WORLD MATH CHALLENGE

One cubic foot of water weighs 62.42 pounds. How much does 1 cubic yard of water weigh? (Hint: 1 cubic yard is equal to 27 cubic feet.)

Number	Size	Weight
1	Cubic foot	62.42 lbs
1	Cubic yard	?

(Turn to page 29 for the answer)

The word *tsunami* is a Japanese word meaning "harbor wave." A tsunami is often called a tidal wave, but that is inaccurate. Tsunamis have nothing to do with regular ocean tides. Normal waves are created by wind blowing across the surface of the water, not by a force rising from the ocean floor.

In addition, natural disasters such as hurricanes and tornadoes have seasons when they are most likely to occur. But tsunamis can happen anytime.

A tsunami is not a single, giant wave. It is a series of waves, sometimes referred to as a "wave train." After the first wave hits shore, more are likely to follow. Sometimes, a second

TSUNAMI ZONE

Some beaches have signs warning visitors to leave the beach in case a tsunami occurs.

IN CASE OF EARTHQUAKE, OR TSUNAMI WARNING, EVACUATE THE BEACHES.

wave arrives only minutes later. Other times, it can take up to an hour for the next wave to strike. Furthermore, the first wave is not always the largest one. Often, the third or fourth wave does the most damage.

Tsunamis don't simply make landfall and stop. Waves often keep rolling until they slam into the next obstacle in their path, typically another piece of land. After Japan was hit, Hawaii prepared for a strike as well. Tsunamis can also rush up rivers. In many ways, they feel like an unstoppable force, but eventually, the water does slow down and stop. Then, the hard work of helping survivors and dealing with the devastation begins.

LEARNING & INNOVATION SKILLS

A group of mathematicians at England's Newcastle University are trying to create a formula to predict tsunamis. They believe the key is in the shape of the first wave while it is still out in deep water. Researchers believe that finding out more about the initial wave will help determine where waves might hit and how destructive they might be. With this information, advance warnings can be issued to residents of an area. That would give them time to find shelter and could save their lives.

CHAPTER THREE
DO THE MATH: HISTORY'S LESSONS

Until recently, tsunamis were rarely in the news or the focus of scientific study. That changed on December 26,

Many homes and businesses in Sumatra were destroyed by the tsunami in 2004.

2004. Deep within the Indian Ocean, a massive earthquake struck when the India tectonic plate slid under the Burma tectonic plate. Trillions of tons of rock were moved in the process, causing the earth to actually shudder under the shifting weight. The quake lasted almost 10 minutes and contained the force of 23,000 atomic bomb explosions.

A killer tsunami was born. In a matter of hours, 11 different countries along the Indian Ocean were hit with huge waves. Reports varied, but some waves were rumored to be as high as 30 feet (9 m). One of the hardest hit areas was Sumatra, one of the islands that makes up Indonesia. Seven hours after hitting Indonesia, the same waves arrived at Somalia in East Africa. They slammed into the shoreline, causing more devastation. By the time the disaster was over, almost 230,000 people had been killed. Countless thousands were missing. Half a million people were injured, and more than 1 million were left homeless.

From Africa all the way to Thailand, people were killed, buildings were reduced to rubble, and entire coastal cities were submerged. Survivors reported that the sound of the incoming wave was like roaring jets or rumbling freight trains.

The world rushed to get supplies, food, water, and medical care to the tsunami victims in Indonesia and other regions. Meanwhile, scientists began studying past tsunami disasters to learn more about this most recent event. They discovered many astonishing facts.

- In 1883, a tsunami followed the huge volcanic explosion on Krakatoa. The waves killed 36,000 people, damaged 132 towns, and completely wiped out 165 more.
- In 1908, a tsunami hit Messina, Italy, with 40-foot-high (12 m) waves, killing about 72,000 people.
- In 1946, an earthquake hit in the Aleutian Islands off the Alaska coast. A wave reported at more than 115 feet (35 m) tall slammed into the coast. The waves continued on to Hawaii, more than 2,000 miles (3,219 km) away. Evacuation orders were issued throughout Hawaii, but because the disaster struck on April 1, many people thought the warnings were an April Fool's joke.

The 1964 tsunami caused flooding and other damage in Alaska and California.

- In 1958, a tsunami hit Lituya Bay in Alaska. The wave reached an incredible 1,739 feet (530 m), but because it was in an isolated bay area, amazingly enough, there was very little damage.
- In 1960, after one of its largest earthquakes on record, Chile was hit with waves up to 38 feet (11.6 m) tall, killing 1,655 and causing more than $550 million in damage. The wave just kept racing through the ocean, next hitting Hawaii, California, and Japan.
- In 1964, a 15-foot-high (4.6 m) tsunami hit Prince William Sound, Alaska, and traveled on to the coast of California. More than 120 people were killed.

REAL WORLD MATH CHALLENGE

Look at the chart below. How long will it take the tsunami to move from Alaska to Hawaii? What is the speed of the tsunami moving from Chile to Japan?

Miles	Speed (miles per hour/mph)	Time (hours)
2,300 miles from Alaska to Hawaii	500 mph	?
10,000 miles from Chile to Japan	?	22 hours

(Turn to page 29 for the answer)

- In 1976, 8,000 people were killed in the southwest Philippines by a tsunami.
- In 1998, Papua New Guinea was struck by a tsunami, and more than 2,000 people were killed.

After a tsunami retreats, and the water flows back off the land, more horrors await the survivors. Cities are devastated, and people are often left without electricity, food, water, clothing, medical care, or housing. Diseases spread quickly.

Entire villages in Papua New Guinea were wiped away by the tsunami in 1998.

Fires erupt in open gas storage tanks. Following the disaster in 2011, Japanese officials feared for the safety of the country's **nuclear reactors**, which had been rocked by the devastation. When a partial **meltdown** occurred, people living near the reactors were told to evacuate. Experts believed it could be decades before the area would be safe to live in again.

LIFE & CAREER SKILLS

Whenever a disaster such as a tsunami strikes, people around the world scramble to help. Local police and fire departments are often first on the scene. Other disaster relief workers may be from the military, such as the U.S. Army and Coast Guard. Volunteers from the American Red Cross or Salvation Army are often present to lend a helping hand. Some workers may be from the Federal Emergency Management Agency (FEMA), a U.S. government agency that provides assistance in all types of disasters. If you like to help others and can work in tough conditions, a career as a disaster relief worker might be the perfect fit for you.

CHAPTER FOUR

DO THE MATH: TOMORROW'S PROTECTION

Knowing when and where a tsunami might hit is tricky. But today, scientists are hard at work trying to figure out how to predict tsunamis. They are getting closer to solving the problem, and with every success, they are able to save more lives.

Scientists use seismographs and other tools to learn more about earthquakes and tsunamis.

In 1807, President Thomas Jefferson established the Survey of the Coast to find out more about the oceans and the weather patterns that affected them. Daily weather maps were published, and in the process, warning systems for hurricanes were developed. As the ocean floor was studied, scientists were able to record vibrations of the ground using the first **seismographs**.

21ST CENTURY CONTENT

One of the most high-tech ways to monitor underwater disturbances is DART, or Deep-Ocean Assessment and Reporting of Tsunamis. **Tsunameters** are electronic devices that are placed on the ocean floor. They detect waves passing through the ocean water. When they perceive an unusually strong or abnormal wave, they send the information to the surface of the water where a buoy floats. Inside the buoy is a package of sophisticated instruments that computes data and sends it to a satellite orbiting in space. That data is sent to scientists throughout the world to let them know if trouble is forming under the ocean surface. If you want to see a DART report, check out *www.ndbc.noaa.gov/dart.shtml.*

REAL WORLD MATH CHALLENGE

The following chart rates the height and effects of waves on a scale of I through XII. Use the chart to answer the questions on the next page.

Category	Wave Height	Effect
I	Not felt	None
II	Scarcely felt	Some people on small boats feel it.
III	Weak	Most people on small boats feel it, and some on the coast see it, but no damage occurs.
IV	Largely observed	People on large and small ships feel it, and most on the coast see it, but no damage occurs.
V	Strong (3-foot waves)	A few people are frightened and run to higher ground. Many small boats go to shore, crash into each other, or even overturn. Flooding and damage to buildings occurs.
VI	Slightly damaging (6-foot waves)	Many people are frightened and run to higher ground. Most small boats go to shore, crash into each other, or overturn. Limited flooding and damage to a few wooden buildings occurs.
VII	Damaging (12-foot waves)	Many people are frightened and try to run to higher ground. Many small boats are damaged. Many wooden buildings are damaged, and some are smashed and/or washed away.
VIII	Heavily damaging (12-foot waves)	A few people are washed away. Most small boats are damaged, and many are washed away. Some large boats move ashore, and a great deal of flooding occurs. Most wooden buildings are smashed, and there is some damage to brick and concrete buildings.
IX	Destructive (26-foot waves)	Many people are washed away. Most small boats are destroyed or washed away. Many large boats move further inland, and some are even destroyed. More damage to brick and concrete buildings occurs.
X	Very destructive (26-foot waves)	People experience panic, and many are washed away. Most large boats move inland, and many cars overturn and float away. Many strong brick buildings are damaged.
XI	Devastating (52-foot waves)	Large fires occur. Cars and other large objects are washed out to sea. Big boulders from the sea bottom move inland, and increased damage to brick and concrete buildings occurs.
XII	Completely devastating (104-foot waves)	Almost all buildings are destroyed or damaged.

REAL WORLD MATH CHALLENGE

Based on the chart on page 22, determine out how high each wave in levels V through XII would be in meters.

Remember:

1 foot = 0.3 meters. Round each meter up to the closest whole number.

Level	Feet	Meters
V	3	?
VI	6	?
VII and VIII	12	?
IX and X	26	?
XI	52	?
XII	104	?

(Turn to page 29 for the answer)

After Alaska's tsunami in 1946, the focus shifted to better understanding these waves and their connection to quakes. The first tsunami warning system was established in 1948 in Hilo, Hawaii. Since then, the warning system has come under the control of the National Oceanic and Atmospheric Administration (NOAA). This agency is responsible for issuing tsunami watches (conditions are likely for a tsunami) and tsunami warnings (a tsunami has been generated). The message is sent to public officials by fax, telephone, and e-mail, and is shared with residents over the radio and television. Sirens may be sounded. Areas at risk have signs posted throughout the region reminding people where to head for safety.

Thanks to underwater monitors, high-tech buoys, and computers, the current tsunami warning system is better than it has ever been. Still, the system does have problems. Warnings have been issued and then turned out to be false alarms. These mishaps create chaos because people evacuate their

Alarms warn people when surrounding areas are at risk of being struck by a tsunami.

homes, jobs, and schools for no reason. Money and time are lost, but more importantly, people will eventually believe that *every* alarm will be false. Such a decision can prove fatal.

Tsunameters are tsunami measuring devices that are positioned in the Pacific Ocean. They alert scientists to developing tsunamis. But what else can be done to deal with tsunamis? Experts offer the following suggestions:

- Install sirens in all cities at risk. (Many countries don't have electricity, so warnings do not reach the people's homes.)
- Install tsunameters in every ocean throughout the world.
- Create seawalls at coastlines to slow down the rush of water.
- Hold regular evacuation drills in threatened cities.
- Offer tsunami education in classrooms around the world.

CHAPTER FIVE
TSUNAMI SURVIVAL TIPS

Perhaps it doesn't seem like knowing about tsunamis is that important where you live. You might not be close to a river, a lake, an ocean, or any coastline. That's probably what 10-year-old Tilly Smith thought when she studied tsunamis with her geography class in Surrey, England, in 2004.

Learning about tsunamis can be useful no matter where you live.

A few weeks later, however, while on vacation with her family in Thailand, Tilly knew exactly how important it was when the ocean suddenly rushed away from the shore. She warned her family that they were in danger, and they ran and told everyone else who would listen. The family went to higher ground and survived the wave that hit only minutes later.

Here are some valuable tips about what you should do if you suspect a tsunami may occur:

1. If you hear a warning or siren, pay attention. It is NOT a joke. Follow the directions of your teacher, parents, or local emergency authorities.

REAL WORLD MATH CHALLENGE

The following tsunamis were some of the worst in history. What is the total number of fatalities? Calculate how many years passed between each tsunami. What is the shortest interval? What is the longest interval?

Year	Location	Number of Fatalities
1707	Japan	30,000
1755	Portugal	70,000
1883	Krakatoa	36,000
1908	Italy	72,000
2004	Indonesia	227,898
2011	Japan	20,352

(Turn to page 29 for the answers)

2. If you see the ocean suddenly retreat from the shore, assume that it is being caused by an approaching wave. Get to safety.

3. If the ocean does anything unusual, assume it's a tsunami. This can include bubbling, hissing, or whistling water.

4. Move quickly, but calmly, to higher ground. Do not stop to pack or take anything with you.

5. Do not go anywhere near the shoreline, even though the first wave has come and gone. More may follow.

6. Know the evacuation routes for your area or community.

7. Do not leave a place of safety until the official "all clear" has been given.

LEARNING & INNOVATION SKILLS

When the huge tsunami hit in the Indian Ocean in 2004, very few animals perished. Why? According to a report from *National Geographic*, before the tsunami arrived, dogs refused to go outside. Many zoo animals went into their shelters and would not come out. Even flamingos left their regular breeding areas to go to higher ground. Alan Rabinowitz, director for science at the Bronx Zoo's Wildlife Conservation Society, explained, "Earthquakes bring vibrational changes on land and in water. . . . Some animals have an acute sense of hearing and smell that allow them to determine something is coming towards them long before humans might know that something is there."

REAL WORLD MATH CHALLENGE ANSWERS

Chapter One

Page 6

There are an average of 5 quakes per day.

2,000 ÷ 365 days per year = 5.48

There are an average of 167 quakes per month.

2,000 ÷ 12 months per year = 166.67

Chapter Two

Page 11

1 cubic yard of water weighs 1,685.34 pounds.

27 cubic feet per cubic yard × 62.42 lbs. per cubic foot = 1,685.34 lbs. per cubic yard

Chapter Three

Page 17

It will take the tsunami 4.6 hours to get from Alaska to Hawaii.

2,300 miles ÷ 500 mph = 4.6 hours

The tsunami from Chile is traveling at 454.55 mph.

10,000 miles ÷ 22 hours = 454.55 mph

Chapter Four

Page 23

Level V: 3 × 0.3 = 0.9, or 1 m

Level VI: 6 × 0.3 = 1.8, or 2 m

Levels VII and VIII: 12 × 0.3 = 3.6, or 4 m

Levels IX and X: 26 × 0.3 = 7.8, or 8 m

Level XI: 52 × 0.3 = 15.6, or 16 m

Level XII: 104 × 0.3 = 31.2, or 31 m

Chapter Five

Page 27

456,250 total fatalities occurred.

30,000 + 70,000 + 36,000 + 72,000 + 227,898 + 20,352 = 456,250

The shortest interval is 7 years.

2011 − 2004 = 7 years

The longest interval is 128 years.

1883 − 1755 = 128 years.

GLOSSARY

friction (FRIK-shuhn) rubbing; the force that slows down objects when they rub against each other

landfall (LAND-fawl) the event of a tsunami, hurricane, or other natural occurrence coming onto land after being over water

meltdown (MELT-doun) the melting of the heated core of a nuclear reactor, resulting in the release of dangerous radiation into the atmosphere

nuclear reactors (NOO-klee-ur ree-AK-turz) large machines that use power created by splitting atoms

oceanographer (oh-shuh-NAH-gruh-fuhr) a scientist who studies the ocean and the plants and animals that live in them

seismographs (SIZE-muh-grafs) instruments that detect earthquakes and measure their power

tectonic plates (tek-TON-ik PLATES) huge landmasses that make up Earth's outer layer; they drift atop a softer material that lies beneath them

tsunameters (tsoo-NAH-muh-turz) electronic devices positioned on the ocean floor to detect waves passing through the water

tsunami (tsoo-NAH-mee) a large, fast-moving series of waves caused by an underwater earthquake or volcano

FOR MORE INFORMATION

BOOKS

Fradin, Judy, and Dennis Fradin. *Witness to Disaster: Tsunamis.* Washington, DC: National Geographic, 2008.

Jennings, Terry. *Earthquakes and Tsunamis.* Mankato, MN: Smart Apple Media, 2010.

Morrison, Taylor. *Tsunami Warning.* Boston: Houghton Mifflin Company, 2007.

WEB SITES

Asian Tsunami Videos

www.asiantsunamivideos.com
Actual video footage of tsunamis, including the 2011 Japanese tsunami and the December 2004 tsunami that struck Thailand, Indonesia, India, and other locations.

National Oceanic and Atmospheric Administration—Tsunami

www.tsunami.noaa.gov
The U.S. government's official site that offers everything you need to know about tsunamis: what they are, detection and warning systems, major tsunami events, a dictionary of tsunami terms, and much more.

Tsunami: The Great Waves

www.weather.gov/om/brochures/tsunami.htm
Visit this U.S. Department of Commerce site to learn how lives are saved, how tsunami warnings are issued, and what you should do in the event of a tsunami.

INDEX

ABOUT THE AUTHOR

Tamra Orr is a full-time writer living in the Pacific Northwest. She has written more than 300 books for readers of all ages. She and her husband, four children, dog, and cat moved to Oregon in 2001. She lives within sight of Mount Saint Helens and visits the coast often, so she pays very close attention to tsunami warning signs.